Discover and
Explore the
Everyday World
With Your Child

Let's Play!

Nancy B. Hertzog, Ph.D.,
Ellen Honeck, Ph.D., &
Barbara Dullaghan, M.Ed.

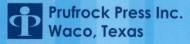

Prufrock Press Inc.
Waco, Texas

Copyright ©2016 Prufrock Press Inc. ● ISBN-13: 978-1-61821-450-8

Edited by Rachel Taliaferro ● Layout design by Raquel Trevino

Prufrock Press Inc., P.O. Box 8813, Waco, TX 76714-8813
Phone: (800) 998-2208 ● http://www.prufrock.com

The Smart Start Series

Let's Play!

To Caregivers:

How to Enjoy This Book With Your Child

Early literacy development begins with spoken language. The more your child talks, the more vocabulary words your child will learn. You will enjoy talking to your child when discussing his or her own ideas! This book promotes early literacy by engaging you and your child in conversation about the book's photographs.

We encourage you to ask three types of open-ended thinking questions:

- **Creative:** Creative questions focus on developing original solutions, products, or processes.

- **Critical:** Critical questions emphasize a dynamic process of questioning and reasoning; may include evaluation of known ideas to produce new ideas.

- **Mathematical:** Mathematical questions engage children in thinking numerically and in patterns; they allow for problem solving, conjectures, and generalizations.

We also encourage you to document or write down your child's responses, read the book again, and see if your child has new and more elaborate ideas. Create a space in your house where you and your child can display the responses to the photographs and revisit them. Elaborating upon or modifying original ideas strengthens your child's disposition to seek alternative responses and to continue to engage in learning.

We hope this book provides you with many ideas for developing your own open-ended questions to engage your child in higher levels of thinking. We would love to hear some of your child's creative ideas about these photographs. Visit the book's webpage at http://www.prufrock.com/Assets/ClientPages/SmartStart.aspx to get more ideas for extending your child's thinking.

Finally, we hope you enjoy the time spent in conversation with your child!

Children play all over the world. In some places it rains more than others. Have you ever played in the rain or in a rain puddle?

Creative Thinking

What types of games could you play outside after the rain?

Critical Thinking

How would this photograph change if it had not rained?

Mathematical Thinking

How do we measure rainfall? How do we measure how deep a puddle is?

The backyard can be a fun place to play. Let's talk about what the boy in the picture is doing in the backyard.

Creative Thinking

Where could the ball go after the boy hits it?

Critical Thinking

What could the boy do to make the ball go short or long distances?

Mathematical Thinking

How could you measure how far the ball travels?

Some children live where it is cold and snow falls on the ground. Let's talk about all of the ways you can play in the snow.

Creative Thinking

What are your ideas for what the kids in the picture can build?

Critical Thinking

If there were no snow, what could you build near your home and what materials could you use?

Mathematical Thinking

How heavy do you think a snowball is?

The boys in the picture are pretending with boxes and props. Let's pretend to play with them.

Creative Thinking
What story do you think the boys
are acting out in the picture?

Critical Thinking
What props and materials would you use
if you could put your ship in the water?

Mathematical Thinking
How would you design a ship to fit
a whole crew of your friends?

PLAYING AT THE PLAYGROUND

This child is playing on a playground. Look at how much fun he is having! Let's talk about how we play on the playground.

Creative Thinking

What are all the ways the boy could play on this piece of equipment?

Critical Thinking

Why do you think he is leaning backward with his eyes closed?

Mathematical Thinking

This piece of equipment can spin. What would happen if he spins too fast, and how could he slow down?

It looks like the kids in the picture are drawing something. Let's talk about what they may be doing.

Creative Thinking

Why do you think
the kids are drawing?

Critical Thinking

Why is the younger child so interested
in the older child's drawing?

Mathematical Thinking

Let's pretend they are drawing a
treasure map—how far do you think
they are from the treasure?

Extension Questions

Playing in the Rain

- What time of year do you think it is in the picture and how can you tell?
- Why isn't there mud everywhere in the picture?
- What will happen when the kids go inside after playing in the rain?

Playing in the Backyard

- What are some other games you could play in the backyard?
- What do you think the boy is thinking in the picture?
- Where would you stand if you wanted to catch the ball?

Playing in the Snow

- What other creations could you make with snow?
- How many ways could the kids measure the size of their snowball?
- These children are working together. What are some other games that you need a friend to play?

Playing in the Box

- If you could play with the boys, what would you add to the story they are acting out?
- How is the boy using the broom?
- Describe a time when you created or acted out a story.

Playing at the Playground

- What are all of the games you could play with your friends at the playground?
- How would you feel after playing on this equipment?
- If you could choose between a playground, a park, or your backyard, where would you like to play and why?

Playing on the Sidewalk

- What do you think the kids were doing before they stopped to draw on the sidewalk?
- What do you think caught their attention?
- Have you ever found or drawn something on the sidewalk before?

For more great ideas, visit our webpage at www.prufrock.com/Assets/ClientPages/SmartStart.aspx